ALL ABOUT WASHINGTON (STATE)

Interesting & Amazing Facts That Everyone Should Know

By Bandana Ojha

Introduction

Filled with up-to-date information, fascinating & fun facts this book "All About Washington (State) - Interesting & Amazing Facts that Everyone Should Know" is the best book for all to find out more about the "Evergreen State". This book would satisfy the children's curiosity and help them to understand why this state is special—and what makes it different from other States. This book gives a story, history, geography, the state symbols & explores many more interesting and fun facts about Washington State. This is a great chance for every kid to expand their knowledge about WA and impress family and friends with all the discovered and never knew before facts.

1. Washington is the northwestern most state of the contiguous United States.

2. Washington is bounded by the Canadian province of British Columbia to the north, the U.S. states of Idaho to the east and Oregon to the south, and the Pacific Ocean to the west.

3. The first recorded European landing on the Washington coast was Spanish Captain Don Bruno de Heceta in 1775.

4. Before Washington became a U.S. state the territory was called Columbia.

5. Washington became the 42nd state of the United States on November 11, 1889.

6. The state of Washington is the only state to be named after a United States president.

7. Washington is the 18th-largest state, and the 13th-most populous state in US.

8. The most Washington's residents live in the Seattle metropolitan area.

9. Washington is not the only name for the state. It is nicknamed as "The Evergreen State" for its abundant evergreen forests.

10. Residents of Washington state are known as "Washingtonians".

11. The USPS abbreviation for Washington is WA.

12. Washington follows Pacific Standard Time abbreviated as PST.

13. The capital of Washington State is Olympia.

14. The State flag is "The Flag of Washington".

15. The Legislature adopted the state flag in 1923, more than thirty years after the state was admitted to the United States.

16. The state flag of Washington is the only flag in the country to have a green background. It is also the only flag to features the face of a president.

17. The State song is "Washington, My Home".

18. The state song was written by Helen Davis, arranged by Stuart Churchill, and became the official state song in 1959.

19. The State seal is "The seal of Washington".

20. The state seal is designed by Charles Talcott shortly before Washington was admitted to the United States in 1889, the seal contains the image of George Washington encircled with "The Seal of the State of Washington" and the date "1889".

21. The State folk song is "Roll On, Columbia, Roll On".

22. The State dance is square dance.

23. The State flower is Coast rhododendron.

24. The State fruit is apple.

25. The State bird is Willow goldfinch.

26. The State fish is Steelhead trout.

27. The State insect is green darner dragonfly.

28. The State Endemic Mammal is Olympic marmot.

29. The State tree is Western hemlock.

30. The State grass is blue bunch wheatgrass.

31. The State vegetable is Walla Walla sweet onion.

32. The State amphibian is Pacific chorus frog.

33. The State oyster is Olympia oyster.

34. The State Marine Mammal is Orca.

35. The State tartan is Washington state tartan.

36. The State fossil is Columbian Mammoth.

37. The State gem is Petrified wood.

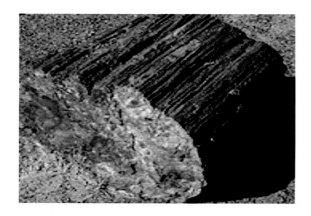

38. The State Ship is Lady Washington.

39. The State waterfall is Palouse Falls.

40. The majestic, 14,410-foot-tall Mount Rainier is the highest point in the state.

41. Lake Chelan's bottom is nearly 400 feet below sea level is the lowest point in the state.

42. With more than 3,000 glaciers, Washington is the most glaciated state in the U.S.

43. Washington's Grand Coulee Dam is the largest dam in the United States.

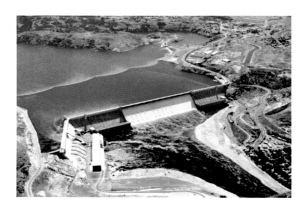

44. Seattle is ranked the most literate city in the country, with the highest percentage of residents with a college degree or higher.

45. Washington is the second most populous state in the west coast and in the western United States after California.

46. Seattle is its most populated city in Washington state. Close to 60 percent of Washington residents live in the Seattle metropolitan area.

47. The U.S. state of Washington has 39 counties.

48. The most populated county in Washington is King County with 2,253,000 residents.

49. The largest county by area in Washington is Okanogan County with 5,268 square miles.

50. Washington State is home to an incredibly diverse range of flora and fauna with 52 percent forest.

51. The state has some of the oldest trees in the country. Several are over a thousand years old and more than 25 feet in circumference.

52. The Washington State Ferry System is the largest in the country and the third largest in the world.

53. The average temperature in Washington is 50.4 °F.

54. Washington is the 29th warmest state in the United States.

55. The warmest temperature ever recorded in Washington was 118 °F on August 5th, 1961.

56. The coldest temperature ever recorded in Washington was -48 °F on December 30th, 1968.

57. It carries more than 25 million passengers each year.

58. Washington State is full of parks; it features 6 national parks and 215 state parks.

59. The three largest cities in Washington are Seattle, Spokane, and Tacoma.

60. Ginkgo Petrified Forest State Park is one of the largest petrified forests in the world.

61. Seattle has the second-highest per capita rate for live music performances in the United States (No-1 is New York City).

62. Seattle's Pier 52 is the busiest ferry terminal in the United States.

63. There are over 40,000 miles of rivers and streams and more than 8,000 lakes in Washington.

64. People in Seattle buy more sunglasses than any other city in the world despite the rain. One reason to account for this may be local people love to do hiking, kayaking, biking, no matter how the weather is!

65. Washington is the United States No.1 producer of apples, raspberries, and sweet cherries.

66. Seattle is nicknamed "the Emerald City" because it's surrounded by so much green.

67. Father's Day originated in Washington in 1910. It began as a statewide holiday, created by Spokane resident Sonora Smart Dodd, who wanted to find a way to honor her father, a civil war veteran.

68. More than 90 percent of U.S. red raspberries and 60 percent of

69. The Washington State Ferry System is the largest Ferry System in the US and the state's number one tourist attraction.

70. Starbucks, the biggest coffee chain in the world was founded in Seattle.

71. The Lunar Rover, the vehicle used by astronauts on the moon was made by Boeing based in Seattle.

72. Seattle and the rest of Washington are home to many tech companies. Microsoft, Amazon, Classmates, Whitepages, Marchex, and Expedia are all based out of Washington. There are also many smaller and startup tech businesses in the state.

73. Hells Canyon, located in Washington, is the deepest gorge in the country. It sits at 8,000 feet deep.

74. Washington's Dungeness is the largest natural sandspit in North America.

75. The first gas station opened in Washington State.

76. With so many forests, Washington is one of the biggest

providers of lumber in the country and around the world.

77. Northgate Mall was the first mall in the United States to be called a mall.

78. Northgate Mall was also the first mall to have public restrooms.

79. Long Beach Washington is the longest continuous beach in the US and the second longest drivable beach in the world.

80. The US Navy has named three of its ships of war after Washington State.

81. The Boeing Company, founded in the Seattle area by William Boeing, was originally a boat company.

82. In World War II, the US government suddenly needed thousands of planes a year, making Boeing the largest employer in Seattle.

83. Seattle has the second-highest per capita rate of live music performances in the United States. New York City is the first.

84. Washington is the 29th wettest state by precipitation (rain and snow) in the United States.

85. Seattle was the first city to have police on bicycles.

86. The world's first soft-serve ice cream machine was in "Olympia Dairy Queen".

87. The Columbia Center building with 76 stories and 937 feet, is Seattle's tallest building and is 12th tallest building in the United States.

88. The only rainforests in the continental U.S. are found on Washington's Olympic Peninsula.

89. Washington State has hosted the World's Fare twice, once in Spokane and once in Seattle.

90. The Evergreen Point Floating Bridge, also known as the 520 Bridge, has 7,710-foot-long floating span and it is the longest floating bridge in the world.

91. Medina is the home of, one of the wealthiest men of the United States, Mr. Bill Gates.

92. Space Needle, Mount Rainier, Olympic National Park, Hoh Rain Forest, Mount St. Helens are the most visited place of the state.

93. Washington was the first state to ban texting and driving to prevent accidents. in 2007.

94. Pike Place Market in Seattle is the longest running farmers market in the US.

95. Harbor Island, WA is the largest man-made island in the US.

96. Harold LeMay from Tacoma had the largest private car collection, owning 3,000 vehicles and thousands of "automobilia" artifacts.

97. The LeMay Collection was listed in the Guinness Book of World Records in 1997 as the largest privately owned car collection in the world.

98. Each summer until his death in 2000, LeMay, his wife Nancy, and their family would open their estate for the annual LeMay Car Show. This

tradition has continued each summer on the last Saturday in August when thousands of visitors could view this vast collection.

99. There are 8,000 lakes are in Washington State.

100. Captain George Vancouver discovered Puget Sound in 1792.

101. One of Washington's most famous attractions is the Space Needle, built in Seattle in 1961 for the World's Fair.

102. It's an observation tower that stands over 600 feet tall.

103. The name Seattle comes from Chief Seattle, or Chief Si'ahl, who was a prominent Native American leader. He played an important role in working to accommodate white settlers in the area.

104. Washington state's Snoqualmie Fall is 100 feet higher than New York's Niagara Falls.

105. Washington state's capitol building was the last state capitol building to be built with a rotunda.

106. Popular games Pictionary, Pickle-ball, and Cranium were all invented in Washington.

107. The Skagit Valley Tulip Festival claims to be Washington's largest festival with over one million visitors and it is held annually in the spring, April 1 to April 30.

108. The Skagit Valley Tulip Festival was officially inaugurated in 1984 by the Mount Vernon Chamber of Commerce. Chamber directors Jerry Diggerness and Joan Houchen saw that people were coming by the thousands to view the tulips and, through a retreat, decided to add

events and festivities to enhance the visitors' trip to the Skagit Valley.

109. In 1994 the Tulip Festival broke off from the Chamber of Commerce and became an entity of its own, eventually opening a separate office and store.

Please check this out:
Our other best-selling books for kids are-
Know about **Sharks**: Interesting & Amazing Facts That Everyone Should Know
Know About **Whales**: Interesting & Amazing Facts That Everyone Should Know
Know About **Dinosaurs**: Interesting & Amazing Facts That Everyone Should Know
Know About **Kangaroos**: Interesting & Amazing Facts That Everyone Should Know
Know About **Penguins**: Interesting & Amazing Facts That Everyone Should Know
Know About **Dolphins** :100 Interesting & Amazing Facts That Everyone Should Know
Know About **Elephant**: Interesting & Amazing Facts That

Everyone Should Know
All About **New York**: Interesting &
Amazing Facts That
Everyone Should Know
All About **New Jersey**: Interesting &
Amazing Facts That
Everyone Should Know
All About **Massachusetts**: 100+
Amazing Facts with Pictures
All About **Florida**: Interesting &
Amazing Facts That
Everyone Should Know
All About **California**: Interesting &
Amazing Facts That
Everyone Should Know
All About **Arizona**: Interesting &
Amazing Facts That
Everyone Should Know
All About **Texas**: Interesting &
Amazing Facts That
Everyone Should Know
All About **Minnesota**: Interesting &
Amazing Facts That

Everyone Should Know
All About **Illinois**: Interesting &
Amazing Facts That
Everyone Should Know
All About **New Mexico**: Interesting &
Amazing Facts That
Everyone Should Know
All About **Canada**: Interesting &
Amazing Facts That
Everyone Should Know
All About **Australia**: Interesting &
Amazing Facts That
Everyone Should Know
All About **Italy**: Interesting &
Amazing Facts That
Everyone Should Know
All About **France**: Interesting &
Amazing Facts That
Everyone Should Know
All About **Japan:** Interesting &
Amazing Facts That
Everyone Should Know

100 Amazing **Quiz Q & A About Penguin**: Never Known Before Penguin Facts

Most Popular **Animal Quiz** book for Kids: 100 amazing animal facts

Quiz Book for Kids: Science, History, Geography, Biology, Computer & Information Technology

English **Grammar** for Kids: Most Easy Way to learn English Grammar

Solar System & Space Science- Quiz for Kids: What You Know About Solar System

English **Grammar Practice** Book for elementary kids: 1000+ Practice Questions with Answers

A to Z of **English Tense**

Made in United States
Orlando, FL
30 December 2024

56707013R00027